Flowers + Tea

A collection of works
by Alexander Ahearn

Flowers + Tea

Publication Date: September 2019
ISBN: 978-1695811409
Photography: Alexander Ahearn
Editing: CT
Layout & Cover Design: Alexander Ahearn

To those who have made, and continue to
make, a difference in my life

Sunflowers, watercolor and micron pen on watercolor paper, 5x7 in (12x17 cm), 2016

Introduction

○   ○   ○   ○   ○

Growing up, I watched my parents drink and enjoy tea. I remember thinking about how bitter any tea was and would put a copious amount of honey in it. Tea was present in my daily life, but I did not think anything of it until I was about eight years old when I had a sencha, a widely-produced style of Japanese green tea, at a local Japanese restaurant. Of course, I ended up putting honey in it again; however, there was something so special about that moment. I wanted to recreate that experience at home and asked my parents if they could find various loose-leaf teas from the store so that we could try them together.

I spent hours researching teas in the hopes of gaining a better understanding of what I was drinking. There was something so intriguing about tea as a beverage and as a plant. After reading all of the tea books that I could get, I began to focus on tea preparation and discerning similarities and differences between tea types and

processing methods. Initially, I gravitated towards Japanese teas and methods of tea preparation. I was, and still am, fascinated by how tea is ingrained in Japanese society and cultural practices. For my first job, I worked at a local, Massachusetts-based bonsai nursery where I was able to learn more about Japanese culture, at least through the world of bonsai. I remember spending hours cleaning and arranging bonsai trees around the nursery, and how I got to interact with so many different kinds of trees each day. Eventually, I became interested in Ikebana, the art of Japanese flower arrangement, and I would make small displays in the nursery. Looking back, my simple arrangements mirror those that I have chosen to put in this book. In November 2010, during my freshman year of high school, I was fortunate enough to travel to Japan with my boss, Teddi, from New England Bonsai Gardens, a few regular customers, and my dad. The trip was mainly a sourcing trip for the nursery, and my boss allowed a small group of customers to join. We traveled to Tokyo, Nikkō, Kyoto, Shikoku Island, and Narita, and met with many bonsai masters. The stunning beauty of Japan, its gracious, hospitable people, and many unforgettable moments filled with laughter had a lasting impact on my life. I am forever grateful to have traveled to Japan when I was that young and to share such a memorable trip with my dad.

My love for tea grew along with a love for baking. I started baking simple recipes when I was about six years old, and knew from an early age that I wanted to pursue a career in the food and beverage industry. I got the opportunity to work at L'Espalier, a local French-American restaurant, as a pastry cook during my last year of high school and through college. Not only was I living my childhood dream, but I also had the opportunity to learn from Cynthia Gold, a renowned tea sommelier, who ran the tea program at L'Espalier. She saw my interest in tea and, when she had time, taught me about the various tea types and preparation methods. She opened my eyes to how good tea can be, and we shared some cups of tea that I still think about today. Her interest in the connection between cooking, baking, and tea fueled my desire to continue to use tea in my baked goods while I was studying Baking &

Pastry Arts at Johnson & Wales University in Providence, Rhode Island, where she also studied.

While in college, I took every opportunity to learn more about tea and its similarities to other beverages, like wine and coffee. This led me to take a foundations of wine class which helped me better understand beverage evaluation and tasting practices, and tasting terminology. Thankfully, my instructor happened to also teach the coffee, tea, and non-alcoholic beverage class, and later became my thesis advisor. She was gracious enough to let me help plan tea tastings for the class to expand the tea experience of my peers. Later, she provided valuable feedback on my thesis about the history of tea and the development of tea culture in the United States.

During this time, I strengthened my understanding of tea tasting and evaluation, and by the end of my degree, I developed a tea evaluation guide that I continue to use as a foundation for improving my palette and my knowledge base. Like wine and coffee, I believe tea requires a method of evaluation for identifying quality and liquor characteristics and discerning differences and similarities between tea types and various processing methods.

I wrote this book with the hope of showing you some of the beauty of tea. It is a representation of the wonders of tea-producing countries, the artistry of tea farmers and producers, and the moments created through tea. Tea is a truly remarkable byproduct of a single plant, Camellia sinensis, and is deeply rooted in the cultures and societies of countries across the world. Drinking and enjoying tea is a unique experience for each one of us. For me, it is pure joy, and it always makes me smile. I hope that this recreation of my recent tea experiences will inspire you in some small way to consider drinking tea as something truly remarkable and that you will take the opportunity to let your mind go in whatever direction the tea takes you.

Sincerely,

My boss, Teddi, and I in Ōmiya, Japan, 2010

Tea: Thunder Dragon Green | Samcholing, Trongsa District, Bhutan | Summer 2017 | Green Tea

White Pages

○　　○　　○　　○　　○

Flowers (left to right): Butterflyweed (Asclepias tuberosa) and Candytuft (Iberis umbellara 'Lilac')

Temi Estate 1st Flush

Steeping parameters:	195°F (90°C)	100ml water	5g tea	20-second steep x5	gaiwan
Liquor color:	Medium - gold	hints of pale orange-yellow
Body:	Medium - body	mild - salivation	slight drying effect
Finish:	Short finish and aftertaste	mild + astringency
Tasting notes:	Fresh nutmeg	dried marjoram	nasturtium	flat-leaf parsley

○　　○　　○　　○　　○

Catch me by surprise

And transport me elsewhere,

Over emptiness.

Tea: Temi Estate 1st Flush | Temi Tea Garden, Temi, South Sikkim, India | Spring 2018 | Black Tea

Flowers: Smooth Hydrangea (Hydrangea arborescens)

Compressed Bai Mu Dan in a Tangerine

Steeping parameters:	175°F (80°C)	100ml water	5g tea	20-second steep x4	gaiwan
Liquor color:	Pale gold	hints of pale orange
Body:	Light body	mild - salivation	slight drying effect
Finish:	Short finish and aftertaste	mild astringency	mild sweetness
Tasting notes:	Orange mint	dried lemon thyme	lemongrass	dried gardenia

○   ○   ○   ○   ○

I run to your beauty,

Leave behind all I hold so dear.

Watch it burn as your presence comes into view.

How can you captivate my attention so?

I extend my arms,

Only to fall at your feet.

I left all that I knew and have met the same ground.

Bare.

Cold, but warmed by your touch.

Tea: Compressed Bai Mu Dan in a Tangerine | Fuding City, Fujian Prefecture, China | Spring 2014 | White Tea

Flowers: Beebalm (Monarda)

Mi Xiang Hong Cha

Steeping parameters:	203°F (95°C)	226ml water	2.5g tea	4-minute steep	teapot
Liquor color:	Medium orange	hints of medium brown and medium - gold
Body:	Medium - body	mild - salivation	medium - drying effect
Finish:	Short + finish and aftertaste	mild + astringency	mild sweetness
Tasting notes:	Dried orange peel	dehydrated fig	apricot	dried magnolia

○   ○   ○   ○   ○

Here you are again,

You never let me know.

We just pass through space

At the same time.

A second shared.

A second passed.

A second reflected upon.

Making me hopeful that we will do this again.

Tea: Mi Xiang Hong Cha | Sun Moon Lake, Yuchi Township, Nantou County, Taiwan | Summer 2018 | Black Tea

Flowers: Franklin Tree (Franklinia alatamaha)

Sagarmatha Gold

Steeping parameters:	195°F (90°C)	226ml water	2.5g tea	3.75-minute steep	teapot
Liquor color:	Medium gold	hints of medium - orange-yellow
Body:	Medium - body	mild - salivation	slight drying effect
Finish:	Short + finish and aftertaste	mild - astringency	mild + sweetness
Tasting notes:	Demerara sugar	butterscotch	carob	malt syrup

○   ○   ○   ○   ○

You became a pigment so eager to please my heart

So enthralled,

That you forgot to shield that which you adore.

I watch as your admiration blooms

Even though you try to hide it.

Tea: Sagarmatha Gold | Ilam, Nepal | Spring 2018 | Black Tea

Flowers: Butterfly Bush (Buddleja)

Asatsuyu Sencha

Steeping parameters:	175°F (80°C)	120ml water	5g tea	1-minute steep	kyusu
Liquor color:	Pale green	hints of pale yellow
Body:	Medium - body	mild - salivation
Finish:	Medium finish and aftertaste	mild - bitterness	mild + sweetness
Tasting notes:	Fresh almond	steamed broccoli	cooked parsnip	butter lettuce

○   ○   ○   ○   ○

Yesterday's flowers bloom for only you,

As if to show you their love.

Guiding you on this path

To create your dream.

Tea: Asatsuyu Sencha | Shizuoka Prefecture, Japan | Spring 2018 | Green Tea

Flowers: Climbing Hydrangea (Hydrangea petiolaris)

Bao Chong Roasted

Steeping parameters:	175°F (80°C)	100ml water	5g tea	20-second steeps x5	gaiwan
Liquor color:	Pale + green	hints of pale + yellow
Body:	Medium - body	mild salivation
Finish:	Short + finish and aftertaste	mild - astringency	mild sweetness
Tasting notes:	Dried magnolia	dried nectarine	cardamom pod	dried gardenia

○   ○   ○   ○   ○

Listen to how I sing just to hear your call.

For years, I have chased after you.

Alone I stand, waiting for your glimmer.

You jumped in.

I can only travel so far.

Tea: Bao Chong Roasted | Taipei County, Taiwan | Spring 2017 | Oolong Tea

Flowers (left to right): Crabapple (Malus 'Adirondack') and American Holly (Ilex opaca)

TRES #21

Steeping parameters:	195°F (90°C)	226ml water	2.5g tea	4-minute steep	teapot
Liquor color:	Medium - orange	hints of pale orange and pale + brown
Body:	Light + body	slight drying effect
Finish:	Medium - finish and aftertaste	mild astringency	mild sweetness
Tasting notes:	Dried grapefruit	pomegranate	muscat grape	dried tangerine

○　　○　　○　　○　　○

You seem so real.

You here with me now,

Beside me.

Right there.

Your smile mimics mine as our fingers intertwine.

Stay for as long as you can.

Tea: TRES #21 | Sun Moon Lake, Yuchi Township, Nantou County, Taiwan | Summer 2018 | Black Tea

Plant: Crabapple (Malus 'Adirondack')

TRES #18

Steeping parameters:	195°F (90°C) I 226ml water I 2.5g tea I 4-minute steep I teapot
Liquor color:	Medium + orange I hints of medium + red-orange and pale brown
Body:	Light + body I slight drying effect
Finish:	Medium - finish and aftertaste I mild astringency I mild sweetness
Tasting notes:	Dried black cherry I allspice I cinnamon stick I dried cranberry

○   ○   ○   ○   ○

Separate yourself from what this is,

Take it for what it is worth;

Nothing to him, but something to you.

Something that changes you,

So that he can one day understand.

Tea: TRES #18 I Sun Moon Lake, Yuchi Township, Nantou County, Taiwan I Summer 2018 I Black Tea

Plant: Flowering Dogwood (Cornus florida)

Kinmokusei

Steeping parameters:	203°F (95°C) I 226ml water I 3g tea I 1.5-minute steep I teapot
Liquor color:	Medium - red-orange I hints of medium orange and pale gold
Body:	Light + body I mild salivation I slight drying effect
Finish:	Short + finish and aftertaste I mild - astringency I mild sweetness
Tasting notes:	Dried apricot I fresh strawberry I agave nectar I red currant

○   ○   ○   ○   ○

Follow me as I run through this garden,

Through a bed of crimson flowers.

Envelop yourself with petals.

Layer them over your heart.

Tea: Kinmokusei I Ureshino, Saga Prefecture, Japan I Summer 2018 I Black Tea with Osmanthus Flowers

Plant: American Elm (Ulmus americana)

Anhui Yellow

Steeping parameters:	195°F (90°C) I 100ml water I 4g tea I 30-second steeps x4 I gaiwan
Liquor color:	Medium gold I hints of pale gold and pale + yellow
Body:	Light + body I mild - salivation I slight drying effect
Finish:	Short + finish and aftertaste I mild - bitterness I mild sweetness
Tasting notes:	Roasted chestnut I watercress I walnut I macadamia honey

○   ○   ○   ○   ○

Be here with me,

Wandering for hours,

Lost in the outline under the sky.

Tea: Anhui Yellow I Anhui Province, China I Spring 2017 I Yellow Tea

Plant: Fern-leaf Japanese Maple (Acer japonicum 'Acontifolium')

GABA Oolong

Steeping parameters:	212°F (100°C)	226ml water	5g tea	1-minute steeps x5	teapot
Liquor color:	Medium + orange	hints of medium + red-orange
Body:	Medium body	medium salivation
Finish:	Medium finish and aftertaste	mild astringency	mild + sweetness
Tasting notes:	Cinnamon stick	pumpkin seed	steamed acorn squash	honey

○   ○   ○   ○   ○

The way in which you meet the sky

Amazes me and gives me guidance;

To see the end of your gaze and find my way.

You move as I do.

We change together through the seasons and even years

Only to see each other in passing.

Tea: GABA Oolong | Lugu Township, Nantou County, Taiwan | Spring 2018 | Oolong Tea

Plant: Coastal Sweet Pepperbush or Summersweet (Clethra alnifolia)

Himalayan Sunrise

Steeping parameters:	203°F (95°C) I 170ml water I 3g tea I 3.5-minute steep I teapot
Liquor color:	Medium - gold I hints of medium - yellow
Body:	Medium body I slight drying effect
Finish:	Medium finish and aftertaste I mild astringency I mild + sweetness
Tasting notes:	Honeycomb I golden raisin I brown sugar I dried wildflowers

○   ○   ○   ○   ○

Subtle reflections of your true self show

As you glide across the night sky,

I watch as the whole world separates from its shadow.

Tea: Himalayan Sunrise I Panchthar District, Nepal I Spring 2016 I Black Tea

Flowers: Mealycup Sage (Salvia farinacea 'Cirrus')

Spring White Buds

Steeping parameters: 185°F (85°C) | 226ml water | 3g tea | 3.5-minute steep | teapot

Liquor color: Pale + gold | hints of pale gold and pale + yellow

Body: Light body | mild salivation | slight drying effect

Finish: Short + finish and aftertaste | mild - astringency | mild sweetness

Tasting notes: Asparagus tips | honeysuckle | dried oregano | fresh almond

○   ○   ○   ○   ○

Part the stillness between the layers of my heart.

Expose the places where my shadows hide.

Tea: Spring White Buds | Ilam, Nepal | Spring 2018 | Black Tea

Plant: Common or Paradise Apple (Malus pumila)

Shanlinxi Oolong

Steeping parameters: 195°F (90°C) | 226ml water | 3g tea | 4-minute steep | teapot

Liquor color: Pale green-yellow | hints of pale green and gold

Body: Medium - body | medium - salivation | slight drying effect

Finish: Medium - finish and aftertaste | mild astringency | mild sweetness

Tasting notes: Honeycrisp apple | gardenia | artichoke | cooked zucchini

○   ○   ○   ○   ○

Temptations extend the space between us.

I look for moments we could share

As our words travel through the same air.

Tea: Shanlinxi | Shanlinxi, Lugu Township, Nantou County, Taiwan | Spring 2018 | Oolong Tea

Flower: Provence Rose (Rosa centifolia)

White Rose

Steeping parameters:	175°F (80°C)	100ml water	3g tea	1-minute steeps x4	gaiwan
Liquor color:	Medium - gold	hints of pale gold and yellow
Body:	Medium - body	mild salivation	slight drying effect
Finish:	Medium - finish and aftertaste	mild - astringency	mild sweetness
Tasting notes:	Dried white peach	agave nectar	dried rose	honeydew melon

○   ○   ○   ○   ○

Please the soul within this bloom.

Carry its heart towards him.

As the bloom starts to burst,

Gaze into his watching eyes.

Blooms blossom from shared roots.

Tea: White Rose | Yunnan Province, China | Spring 2017 | White Tea

Plant: Silver Wormwood (Artemisia ludoviciana)

Jalinga White Tips

Steeping parameters:	175°F (80°C)	100ml water	3g tea	20-second steeps x5	gaiwan
Liquor color:	Pale + gold	hints of pale gold and yellow
Body:	Medium - body	mild salivation	slight drying effect
Finish:	Short + finish and aftertaste	mild - astringency	mild sweetness
Tasting notes:	Dried apricot	brown sugar	dried orange peel	honeysuckle

○   ○   ○   ○   ○

Bring me along with you.

Look back at me and meet my gaze

Then look at the fields ahead.

Tea: Jalinga White Tips | Assam, India | Summer 2017 | White Tea

Flowers: White Wood Aster (Eurybia divaricata)

Thunder Dragon Green

Steeping parameters:	175°F (80°C) I 100ml water I 5g tea I 20-second steeps x5 I gaiwan
Liquor color:	Pale + green-gold I hints of pale yellow and green
Body:	Medium body I mild - salivation I slight drying effect
Finish:	Short + finish and aftertaste I mild bitterness I mild - sweetness
Tasting notes:	Dried tarragon I steamed bok choy I coriander seed I lemon zest

O   O   O   O   O

We will meet eventually,

As time only pushes us together.

Each year the same flowers grow,

And signal that time has, in fact, passed.

You change to only be brought back here,

Where I will pass you again.

Tea: Thunder Dragon Green I Samcholing, Trongsa District, Bhutan I Summer 2017 I Green Tea

Plant: White Oak (Quercus alba)

Oolong Nakai

Steeping parameters:	203°F (95°C)	226ml water	2.5g tea	1-minute steep	teapot
Liquor color:	Medium gold	hints of pale orange and pale brown
Body:	Medium body	mild salivation	slight drying effect
Finish:	Short + finish and aftertaste	mild - astringency	mild sweetness
Tasting notes:	Dried apricot	oak wood	roasted chestnut	amber caramel

○   ○   ○   ○   ○

Be still and pose for me,

As I once did for you.

I can only see you for such a short time

Before things change and I have moved on.

For I will always be here; standing.

Seasons pass as I wait; you finally appear

And stare at me as you did last year.

Tea: Oolong Nakai | Wazuka Prefecture, Japan | Summer 2017 | Oolong Tea

Plant: Full Moon Maple (Acer shirasawanum 'Aureum')

Matcha Suzume

Steeping parameters:	175°F (80°C) | 60ml water | 1.5g tea | whisk | chawan
Liquor color:	Medium green | hints of medium + green
Body:	Medium body | mild salivation | slight drying effect
Finish:	Medium finish and aftertaste | mild - bitterness | mild + sweetness
Tasting notes:	Steamed spinach | cooked green beans | snap peas | nori

○　　○　　○　　○　　○

Your breath warms the space between us.

Thoughts race through my mind,

As I try to find ways to see you.

Days go by,

Yet the warmth you left remains.

Tea: Matcha Suzume | Uji, Kyoto Prefecture, Japan | Spring 2018 | Green Tea

Plant and Flowers (left to right): Eastern Woodfern (Dryopteris marginalis), Swamp Milkweed (Asclepias incarnata 'Ice Ballet'), and Yarrow (Achillea 'Coronation Gold')

Arun White

Steeping parameters:	175°F (80°C) I 226ml water I 5g tea I 1-minute steeps x2 I teapot
Liquor color:	Pale gold I hints of pale - gold and pale yellow
Body:	Light + body I mild salivation
Finish:	Short finish and aftertaste I mild - astringency I mild + sweetness
Tasting notes:	Nectar I dried nectarine I linden honey I straw

○   ○   ○   ○   ○

Fragments converge in a moment,

Accented by a color we chose.

Sudden eruptions of pigment,

Overtake one's soul.

Tea: Arun White I Maetang District, Chiang Mai, Thailand I Spring 2018 I White Tea

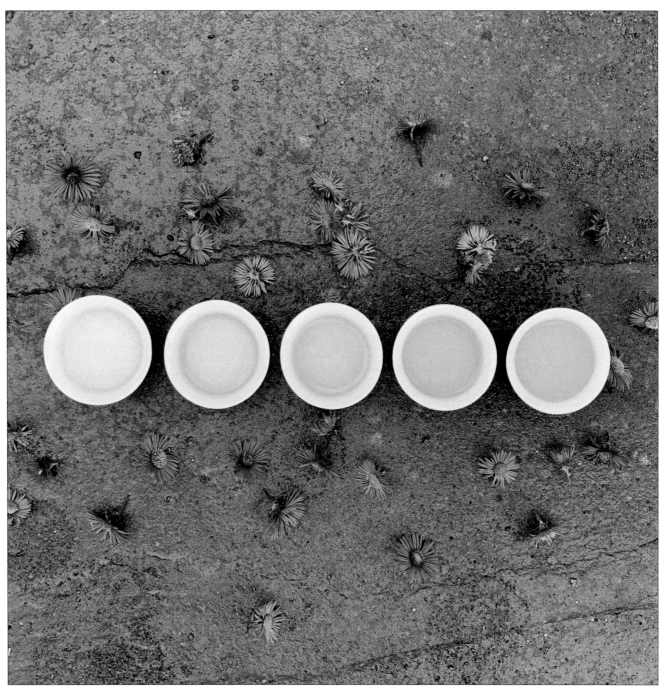

Flowers: New England Aster 'Purple Dome' (Symphyotrichum novae-angliae 'Purple Dome')

Darjeeling 2nd Flush Muscatel Valley Estate

Steeping parameters:	203°F (95°C)	100ml water	5g tea	5 steeps	gaiwan
Liquor color:	Medium - gold	hints of pale yellow and pale gold
Body:	Light + body	mild salivation	slight drying effect
Finish:	Short + finish and aftertaste	mild - astringency	mild sweetness

Tasting note changes over five steeps

1st (20 seconds):	Dried orange peel	dried jasmine	orange blossom honey
2nd (30 seconds):	Celery leaf	coriander seed	green grape
3rd (40 seconds):	Dried oregano	dried basil	dried green apple
4th (50 seconds):	Macadamia	orange peel	green grape skin
5th (60 seconds):	Fennel seed	dried ginger	dried apricot

○   ○   ○   ○   ○

Escape my grasp.

Hide within the flowers,

So that you share your beauty.

Tea: Darjeeling 2nd Flush Muscatel Valley Estate | West Bengal, India | Summer 2018 | Black Tea

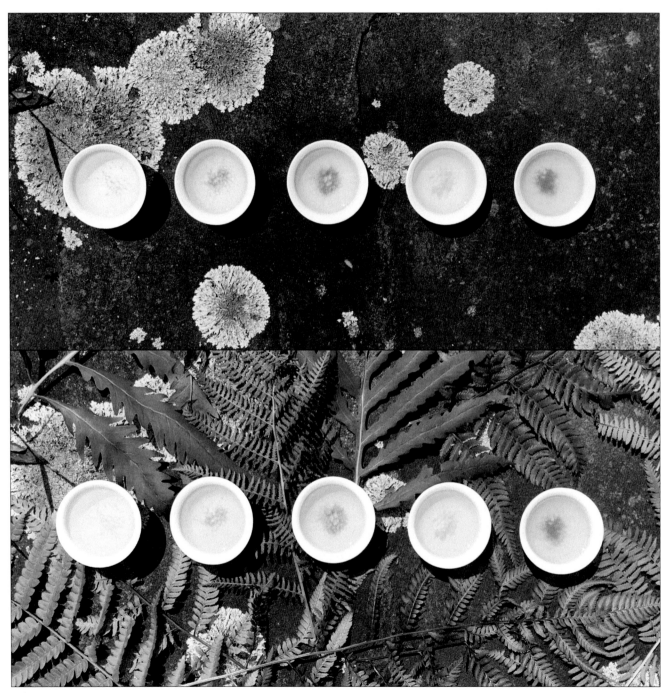

Plants (left to right): Sensitive Fern (Onoclea sensibilis), Eastern Woodfern (Dryopteris marginalis), and Japanese Painted Fern (Athyrium niponicum 'Pictum')

Miyabi Shincha

Steeping parameters:	175°F (80°C)	60ml water	5g tea	5 steeps	kyusu
Liquor color:	Medium - green-yellow	hints of pale green
Body:	Light body	mild salivation	slight drying effect
Finish:	Short + finish and aftertaste	mild - bitterness	mild sweetness

Tasting note changes over five steeps

1st (25 seconds):	Steamed spinach	fresh asparagus	toasted cashew
2nd (10 seconds):	Steamed chard	steamed collard greens	dried raspberry
3rd (15 seconds):	Endive	cooked chard	cooked asparagus
4th (15 seconds):	Dried nectarine	dried green apple	leek
5th (20 seconds):	Water chestnut	cooked spinach	dried lilies

○   ○   ○   ○   ○

This one meeting.

One look.

Separated by only the space between our breaths.

Tea: Miyabi Shincha | Fukuoka Prefecture, Japan | Spring 2018 | Green Tea

Flowers: Sweet Autumn Clematis (Clematis paniculata)

Darjeeling 2ⁿᵈ Flush Rohini Estate

Steeping parameters: 195°F (90°C) | 226ml water | 2.5g tea | 4-minute steep | teapot

Liquor color: Medium brown | hints of medium orange and medium gold

Body: Medium + body | mild salivation | slight drying effect

Finish: Medium finish and aftertaste | mild - astringency | mild + sweetness

Tasting notes: Dried apricot | brown butter | toasted wheat | dried rose

○   ○   ○   ○   ○

The breath of this creature lingers next to mine.

Shared silence consumes the air,

Only to be filled with a faint warmth.

Forms appear and manifest themselves

In the slivers of light between us.

Tea: Darjeeling 2nd Flush Rohini Estate | West Bengal, India | Summer 2018 | Black Tea

Flowers: Wood Forget-me-not (Myosotis sylvatica)

Soba Cha

Steeping parameters: 212°F (100°C) | 226ml water | 6g tea | 1-minute steep | teapot

Liquor color: Pale gold-yellow | hints of pale brown and pale yellow

Body: Light body

Finish: Short + finish and aftertaste | mild + sweetness

Tasting notes: Wheat kernels | toasted almond | oats | toasted cinnamon stick

O   O   O   O   O

As I run my hand through this field,

Filled with thousands of flowers.

Something grabs my hand,

Pulling me into this memory

Under the beauty of others.

Blind to time,

I search for reality.

Only to find a new me.

Tea: Soba Cha | Nagano Prefecture, Japan | Tisane (Herbal Tea)

Flowers: White Snakeroot (Ageratina altissima)

Uji No Sato Sencha

Steeping parameters:	175°F (80°C) I 120ml water I 5g tea I 1-minute steeps x2 I kyusu
Liquor color:	Pale green I hints of pale - green and pale yellow
Body:	Light + body I mild salivation
Finish:	Medium - finish and aftertaste I mild - bitterness I mild sweetness
Tasting notes:	Steamed arugula I cooked chestnut I snap peas I dried gardenia

○   ○   ○   ○   ○

A softness carries the wind through this room

Heartened by the laughter of the forest which built this house.

As the years pass, comforted by the joys of others,

You can still hear the forest through the wind.

Tea: Uji No Sato Sencha I Uji, Kyoto Prefecture, Japan I Spring 2018 I Green Tea

Pink Lilies, watercolor and micron pen on watercolor paper, 5x7 in (12x17 cm), 2017

More Photos

○   ○   ○   ○   ○

Tea: Bao Chong Roasted I Taipei County, Taiwan I Spring 2017 I Oolong Tea

Tea: Jalinga White Tips | Assam, India | Summer 2017 | White Tea

Flowers: Franklin Tree (Franklinia alatamaha)

Flowers: Franklin Tree (Franklinia alatamaha)

Tea: Darjeeling 2nd Flush Rohini Estate | West Bengal, India | Summer 2018 | Black Tea

Flowers: Sweet Autumn Clematis (Clematis paniculata)

Tea: Matcha Suzume | Uji, Kyoto Prefecture, Japan | Spring 2018 | Green Tea

Tea: Anhui Yellow | Anhui Province, China | Spring 2017 | Yellow Tea

Tea: Gu Zhu Zi Zhun (Purple Bamboo Shoot) | Hu Zhou City, Zhejiang Province, China | Spring 2018 | Green Tea

Black Pages

○   ○   ○   ○   ○

Flowers: Common Lilac (Syringa vulgaris)

Oriental Beauty

Steeping parameters:	203°F (95°C) I 100ml water I 3g tea I 30-second steeps x6 I gaiwan
Liquor color:	Medium + orange I hints of medium gold and pale + yellow
Body:	Light + body I mild salivation
Finish:	Short + finish and aftertaste I mild sweetness
Tasting notes:	Dried lilac I honeycomb I dried rose I quince

○   ○   ○   ○   ○

A haze enters my chest as you stand there.

Warmth escapes my lungs as you speak,

As my heart strains to release this excitement.

Tea: Oriental Beauty I Hsinchu County, Taiwan I Summer 2016 I Oolong Tea

Flowers: Flowering Quince (Chaenomeles 'Jet Trail')

Zairai Kamairicha

Steeping parameters:	175°F (80°C) | 120ml water | 5g tea | 1-minute steeps x3 | kyusu
Liquor color:	Pale green | hints of pale + green and pale - yellow
Body:	Light body | mild salivation
Finish:	Short + finish and aftertaste | mild bitterness | mild sweetness
Tasting notes:	Nasturtium | toasted hazelnut | water chestnut | dried magnolia

○   ○   ○   ○   ○

I know that you are still there

Hidden in this dense forest in front of me.

The grass brushes against my feet

Guiding me towards you.

Tea: Zairai Kamairicha \| Gokase, Miyazaki Prefecture, Japan \| Spring 2018 \| Green Tea

Flowers (top to bottom): White Peony (Paeonia 'La Lorraine') and American Elderberry (Sambucus canadensis)

Jade Mountain

Steeping parameters:	195°F (90°C)	90ml water	3g tea	25-second steeps x8	teapot
Liquor color:	Pale + green-yellow	hints of pale green and pale yellow
Body:	Light + body	mild + salivation
Finish:	Short finish and aftertaste	mild + sweetness
Tasting notes:	Dried peony	dried ginger	dried lemon peel	lilac

○   ○   ○   ○   ○

I have always followed you

Along the edge of this path.

I tripped and realized how wide the path really is.

Tea: Jade Mountain | Nantou County, Taiwan | Winter 2018 | Oolong Tea

Flowers: Double Weeping Cherry (Prunus pendula 'Pendula Rosea')

Marushige Shimizu Kabusecha

Steeping parameters:	175°F (80°C)	120ml water	5g tea	1-minute steeps x3	kyusu
Liquor color:	Medium - green	hints of medium green and pale + yellow
Body:	Light + body	mild salivation
Finish:	Medium - finish and aftertaste	mild - bitterness	mild + sweetness
Tasting notes:	Cooked arugula	toasted almond	collard greens	steamed chard

○   ○   ○   ○   ○

Empty this hollowness from my words

So only truth remains.

Tea: Kabusecha | Suizawa Village, Yokkaichi City, Mie Prefecture, Japan | Spring 2018 | Green Tea

Flowers: Rhododendron (Rhododendron 'Elite')

Oolong Kiriyama

Steeping parameters:	175°F (80°C) I 120ml water I 4g tea I 1-minute steeps x2 I kyusu
Liquor color:	Medium gold I hints of pale green and pale + yellow
Body:	Light + body I mild salivation
Finish:	Short + finish and aftertaste I mild - bitterness I mild + sweetness
Tasting notes:	Dried magnolia I dried lemon zest I steamed asparagus I narcissus

○   ○   ○   ○   ○

You have already reached the end.

I wonder how you knew which one to choose;

Which path, page, side.

Tea: Oolong Kiriyama I Makinohara, Shizuoka Prefecture, Japan I Spring 2018 I Oolong Tea

Flowers: Pink and Sweet Azalea (Rhododendron 'Pink And Sweet')

Gu Zhu Zi Zhun

Steeping parameters:	175°F (80°C)	100ml water	3g tea	20-second steeps x5	gaiwan
Liquor color:	Pale - green	hints of pale green and pale - yellow
Body:	Light + body	mild salivation	slight drying effect
Finish:	Short finish and aftertaste	mild - sweetness
Tasting notes:	Bean sprout	green beans	microgreens	dried lilies

O   O   O   O   O

As you walk along the path I once knew,

The way in which you part the field amazes me;

Effortlessly tracing the thorns on the rose beside you.

Tea: Gu Zhu Zi Zhun (Purple Bamboo Shoot) | Hu Zhou City, Zhejiang Province, China | Spring 2018 | Green Tea

Flowers: Pinxter Flower or Pinxterbloom Azalea (Rhododendron periclymenoides)

De Jian Long Zhu

Steeping parameters: 175°F (80°C) | 100ml water | 3g tea | 20-second steeps x4 | gaiwan

Liquor color: Pale green | hints of pale - green and pale - yellow

Body: Light + body | mild salivation | slight drying effect

Finish: Short - finish and aftertaste | mild - bitterness | mild sweetness

Tasting notes: Steamed zucchini | cucumber | watercress | fresh almond

○   ○   ○   ○   ○

Eager desire draws me inward

Unravels my heart;

Giving me the freedom to fall freely.

Tea: De Jian Long Zhu | Guizhou Province, China | Spring 2019 | Green Tea

Flowers: Spirea or Bridalwreath (Spirea 'Snowmound')

Wood Dragon

Steeping parameters:	212°F (100°C)	100ml water	3g tea	45-second steeps x4	gaiwan
Liquor color:	Medium + orange-gold	hints of medium - orange and pale + gold
Body:	Medium body	mild salivation
Finish:	Short + finish and aftertaste	mild + sweetness
Tasting notes:	Pine nut	vanilla bean pod	cashew	shelled peanut

○   ○   ○   ○   ○

Silence drifts over my thoughts of you

And fills with the sound of your voice.

All so familiar since our eyes met.

Tea: Wood Dragon | Nantou County, Taiwan | Spring 2017 | Oolong Tea

Flowers: Japanese Flowering Cherry (Prunus serrulata 'Kanzan')

Bai Mu Dan

Steeping parameters:	175°F (80°C)	100ml water	3g tea	45-second steeps x5	gaiwan
Liquor color:	Pale gold	hints of pale - gold and pale yellow
Body:	Light + body	mild salivation	slight drying effect
Finish:	Short finish and aftertaste	mild sweetness
Tasting notes:	Bay leaf	nettle	dried honeysuckle	sunflower honey

○   ○   ○   ○   ○

Your eyes pierce through the dark,

And illuminate mine;

Connecting a chain in this haze.

Tea: Bai Mu Dan | Fujian Province, China | Spring 2018 | White Tea

Plant: Eastern Red Cedar (Juniperus virginiana)

Dark Roasted Hojicha

Steeping parameters: 195°F (90°C) | 120ml water | 5g tea | 1-minute steeps x3 | kyusu

Liquor color: Medium + orange-gold | hints of medium brown and medium gold

Body: Light + body | mild salivation

Finish: Medium - finish and aftertaste | mild sweetness

Tasting notes: Toasted brown rice | malt syrup | demerara sugar | buckwheat

     o   o   o   o   o

I have been waiting years for you.

Our eyes soon meet, and you take me by surprise.

Your face mirrors mine.

You say a few words, and I can only smile.

Tea: Dark Roasted Hojicha | Kyoto Prefecture, Japan | Spring 2018 | Green Tea

Flowers: Common Blue Violet (Viola soraria) and Sweet White Violet (Viola blanda)

Unshaded Matcha

Steeping parameters:	175°F (80°C) I 65ml water I 2g tea I whisk - 45 seconds I chawan
Liquor color:	Pale green I hints of pale - green and medium - green
Body:	Light + body I mild salivation
Finish:	Short + finish and aftertaste I mild bitterness I mild + sweetness
Tasting notes:	Cooked spinach I turnip I fresh almond I daikon

○   ○   ○   ○   ○

As leaves escape their homes,

I run after them to find my own;

To be charmed by the same wind,

Onto another path.

Tea: Unshaded Matcha I Hoshinomura, Fukuoka Prefecture, Japan I Spring 2018 I Green Tea

Flowers: Norway Maple (Acer platanoides)

Ruyi Bingcha

Steeping parameters:	37°F (3°C) I 450ml water I 10g tea I 12-hour cold brew
Liquor color:	Medium + gold I hints of medium gold and pale + orange-yellow
Body:	Medium - body I slight drying effect
Finish:	Short + finish and aftertaste I mild - astringency I mild sweetness
Tasting notes:	Cocoa husk I wheat kernels I dry roasted peanut I white oak

○   ○   ○   ○   ○

Warmth traces the features on your face,

Meeting the shadow cast down by your hazel eyes

Which now become gold by a joyful heart.

Tea: Ruyi Bingcha I Yunnan Province, China I Summer/Fall 2017 I Black Tea

Flowers: Flowering Dogwood (Cornus florida 'Barton')

Bai Hao Yin Zhen

Steeping parameters: 175°F (80°C) | 100ml water | 5g tea | 30-second steeps x6 | gaiwan

Liquor color: Pale gold-yellow | hints of pale - green and pale - yellow-green

Body: Light body | slight drying effect

Finish: Short + finish and aftertaste | mild sweetness

Tasting notes: Straw | dried honey | dried magnolia | honeysuckle

○   ○   ○   ○   ○

After hearing your voice,

My mind is as clear as the pitch of my heart.

Tea: Bai Hao Yin Zhen | Fujian Province, China | Spring 2018 | White Tea

Flowers: Rhododendron (Rhododendron 'Black Satin') and Catawba Rhododendron (Rhododendron catawbiense boursalt)

Tamaryokucha

Steeping parameters:	175°F (80°C) | 100ml water | 4g tea | 1-minute steeps x3 | kyusu
Liquor color:	Medium - green | hints of pale + green and pale - yellow
Body:	Light body | mild salivation
Finish:	Short finish and aftertaste | mild bitterness | mild - sweetness
Tasting notes:	Brussels sprouts | white sesame seeds | steamed arugula | pine nut

○   ○   ○   ○   ○

Reflect back at me.

Let me see your wide eyes.

See me, as I you.

Tea: Tamaryokucha | Ureshino, Saga Prefecture, Japan | Spring 2018 | Green Tea

Flowers: Crabapple (Malus 'Adams')

Shikoku Goishi Cha

Steeping parameters: 195°F (90°C) | 120ml water | 3g tea | 1-minute steeps x3 | kyusu

Liquor color: Medium orange-yellow | hints of pale + gold and pale + yellow

Body: Light + body | mild salivation | slight drying effect

Finish: Medium - finish and aftertaste | mild - astringency | mild sweetness

Tasting notes: Dried red plum | date | ripe nectarine | caramelized hazelnut

○   ○   ○   ○   ○

Welcome back to this place

That holds all our memories.

I come back often,

Without you.

To give me something to believe in.

Tea: Shikoku Goishi Cha | Ôtoyo, Kôchi Prefecture, Shikoku Island, Japan | Spring 2016 | Fermented Tea

Flowers: Crabapple (Malus 'Adirondack')

Kurundu Estate Ceylon

Steeping parameters:	212°F (100°C)	226ml water	2.5g tea	4-minute steep	teapot
Liquor color:	Medium + orange	hints of pale orange-red and pale + gold
Body:	Light + body	slight drying effect
Finish:	Medium - finish and aftertaste	mild + astringency	mild sweetness
Tasting notes:	Nectarine	orange peel	malt syrup	dried apricot

○   ○   ○   ○   ○

Looking down the tunnel created by these trees,

You run towards the faint light at the end, and

Realize that it is just the sun rising over an unknown path.

Tea: Kurundu Estate Ceylon | Ruhuna District, Sri Lanka | Summer 2017 | Black Tea

Plant and Flowers (left to right): American Boxwood (Buxus sempervirens), Paperwhite (Narcissus papyraceus), and Daffodil (Narcissus)

Yamashita Gyokuro

Steeping parameters:	140°F (60°C) I 60ml water I 7g tea I 2-minute steeps I kyusu
Liquor color:	Medium green-yellow I hints of pale + green and pale - yellow
Body:	Medium - body I mild salivation
Finish:	Long finish and aftertaste I mild bitterness I mild sweetness
Tasting notes:	Cooked spinach I cooked parsnip I dried gardenia I artichoke

○   ○   ○   ○   ○

You are so caught up with this,

The blur and the rush.

Look at me.

Meet my gaze and stop.

There is something more about you,

Concealed by your smile.

Tea: Yamashita Gyokuro I Kyotanabe, Kyoto Prefecture, Japan I Spring 2018 I Green Tea

Flowers: Loebner Magnolia (Magnolia x loebneri)

Li Shan Black

Steeping parameters:	212°F (100°C) I 100ml water I 5g tea I 20-second steeps x5 I gaiwan
Liquor color:	Medium + red-orange I hints of medium orange and pale + gold
Body:	Medium body I mild salivation I slight drying effect
Finish:	Medium - finish and aftertaste I mild astringency I mild + sweetness
Tasting notes:	Agave nectar I dried apricot I cocoa nib I dried magnolia

○　　○　　○　　○　　○

Light breaks the silence hidden between the trees, and

The world scatters as it spreads.

Tea: Li Shan Black I Lishan, Hualien County, Taiwan I Summer 2018 I Black Tea

Plant: Coral Bark Maple (Acer palmatum 'Sango Kaku')

Kawane Sencha

Steeping parameters:	175°F (80°C)	120ml water	5g tea	1-minute steeps x2	kyusu
Liquor color:	Pale + green	hints of pale green and pale - yellow
Body:	Light + body	mild salivation
Finish:	Short finish and aftertaste	mild + bitterness	mild - sweetness
Tasting notes:	Steamed chard	dried gardenia	narcissus	cooked endive

o   o   o   o   o

This feeling rushes over me as I look away.

I adjust to the starkness of the path ahead.

Tea: Kawane Sencha | Shizuoka Prefecture, Japan | Spring 2018 | Green Tea

Plant: Red Spruce (Picea rubens)

Tongmu Reserve Lapsang Souchong

Steeping parameters:	212°F (100°C) I 226ml water I 2.5g tea I 4-minute steep I teapot
Liquor color:	Medium + orange-red I hints of pale + orange and pale + gold
Body:	Light + body I slight drying effect
Finish:	Short + finish and aftertaste I mild astringency I mild sweetness
Tasting notes:	Resin I red currant I pine needles I dried lilac

○   ○   ○   ○   ○

It rained while the surroundings hummed to their own song.

The rain joined and sang to the sway of the trees.

Tea: Tongmu Reserve Lapsang Souchong I Fujian Province, China I Spring 2017 I Black Tea

Plant: River Birch (Betula nigra)

Darjeeling 2nd Flush Castleton Estate

Steeping parameters:	195°F (90°C) I 226ml water I 2.5g tea I 4-minute steep I teapot
Liquor color:	Medium - orange-gold I hints of pale orange and pale + gold
Body:	Light + body I slight drying effect
Finish:	Short + finish and aftertaste I mild + astringency I mild - sweetness
Tasting notes:	Cedar I barley I dried orange peel I walnut

○   ○   ○   ○   ○

Curious eyes linger on your face.

They watch as you smile,

To flicker when you do.

Tea: Darjeeling 2nd Flush Castleton Estate I West Bengal, India I Summer 2018 I Black Tea

Flowers: Lily of the Valley (Convallaria majalis)

Mi Lan Xiang

Steeping parameters:	203°F (95°C)	100ml water	3g tea	20-second steeps x6	gaiwan
Liquor color:	Medium - orange-yellow	hints of pale orange-gold and pale gold
Body:	Light + body	mild + salivation
Finish:	Medium - finish and aftertaste	mild astringency	mild sweetness
Tasting notes:	Lily of the valley	dried peony	dried clementine	mimosa honey

O   O   O   O   O

Stare carelessly into the distance.

I watch and smile as your eyes meet the skyline,

Reflecting its beauty onto your eyes.

Tea: Mi Lan Xian | Guangdong Province, China | Spring 2016 | Oolong Tea

Plant: Variegated Japanese Maple (Acer palmatum 'Uzen Nishiki')

Sencha Yabukita

Steeping parameters:	175°F (80°C)	120ml water	5g tea	1-minute steeps x3	kyusu
Liquor color:	Pale + green	hints of pale - green and pale - green-yellow
Body:	Light + body	mild salivation
Finish:	Medium finish and aftertaste	mild - bitterness	mild sweetness
Tasting notes:	Fresh spinach	artichoke heart	larch	dried lemon zest

○   ○   ○   ○   ○

There was a time when you would sing in this house.

You opened your heart and enlarged mine.

I still hear you sing as you beat in my heart.

Tea: Sencha Yabukita | Shizuoka Prefecture, Japan | Spring 2018 | Green Tea

Flowers: Redvein Enkianthus (Enkianthus campanulatus)

Anxi Tie Guan Yin

Steeping parameters:	195°F (90°C) I 100ml water I 3g tea I 30-second steeps x5 I gaiwan
Liquor color:	Pale + green I hints of pale + yellow and pale green
Body:	Light + body I mild salivation
Finish:	Short finish and aftertaste I mild - bitterness I mild - sweetness
Tasting notes:	Quince I dried gardenia I dried peony I brazil nut

○   ○   ○   ○   ○

The music plays as we talk more.

It softens in the distance

As we walk under the light of the moon.

Tea: Anxi Tie Guan Yin I Fujian Province, China I Spring 2018 I Oolong Tea

Flowers: Japanese Dappled Willow (Salix integra 'Hakuro-Nishiki')

Sparrow's Tongue

Steeping parameters:	175°F (80°C) | 100ml water | 3g tea | 25-second steeps x4 | gaiwan
Liquor color:	Pale + green | hints of pale - green and medium - yellow-green
Body:	Light body | mild salivation | slight drying effect
Finish:	Short finish and aftertaste | mild - bitterness | mild sweetness
Tasting notes:	Steamed artichoke | fresh bok choy | dried lilies | alfalfa

○   ○   ○   ○   ○

I can't seem to remember where I first saw this flower.

I tripped over roots to follow it when I was younger,

Stunned by its yellow hue.

Tea: Sparrow's Tongue | Hwagae Valley, Korea | Spring 2019 | Green Tea

Tea Flowers, watercolor, black tea, and micron pen on watercolor paper, 5x7 in (12x17 cm), 2017

More Photos

○ · ○ ○ ○ ○

Flowers: Flowering Quince (Chaenomeles 'Jet Trail')

Flowers: Japanese Flowering Cherry (Prunus serrulata 'Kanzan')

Flowers: Rhododendron (Rhododendron 'Black Satin') and Catawba Rhododendron (Rhododendron catawbiense)

Flowers: Crabapple (Malus 'Adams')

Plant: Eastern Red Cedar (Juniperus virginiana)

Plant: Variegated Japanese Maple (Acer palmatum 'Uzen Nishiki')

Flowers: White Peony (Paeonia 'La Lorraine')

Flowers: Redvein Enkianthus (Enkianthus campanulatus)

Bloom for Me, 2017

Acknowledgments

Sebastian Beckwith and Ana Dane, thank you for all of the great conversations and laughs over incredible cups of tea. Thank you for your continuous support and motivation to follow my dreams.

Cynthia Gold, thank you for showing me the beauty of tea all of those years ago. I will always remember sharing tea with you and cherish those unforgettable moments forever. Words cannot explain how thankful that I am that you noticed my interest in tea — I would not be where I am today without your help.

Karin and David Hagan, thank you for sharing so many cups of tea with me and for encouraging me over the years.

Katrina Herold, thank you for helping me strengthen my tea knowledge and for pushing me to learn more about beverages. Thank you for supporting my desire to learn more and for providing me with opportunities to teach others.

Mom and Dad, there are not enough words to explain how grateful I am to have you two as my parents. Thank you for encouraging me to always be curious and excited about what I am interested in. Thank you for guiding me to get where I am and for always being by my side.

Teddi and Hitoshi, thank you for being such important people in my life.

Samantha Tilney, thank you for sharing your love of tea with me and cheers to many more cups of tea.

David Slayback, thank you for pushing me to finish this book and for sharing many laughs over cups of tea.

Special thanks to Kellen Andrilenas, Ethan Apter, Linda Barrows, Chase Ennis, Jo Johnson, Broderick Kaplan, Virginia Utermohlen Lovelace, Marzi Pecen, Sara Shackett, Rie Tulali, Anna Ye, and everyone who shared a cup of tea with me over the years.

Made in the USA
San Bernardino,
CA